EXTREME SPORTS EVENTS

ARROWHEAD 135

ANTHONY K. HEWSON

SportsZone
An Imprint of Abdo Publishing
abdobooks.com

abdobooks.com

Published by Abdo Publishing, a division of ABDO, PO Box 398166, Minneapolis, Minnesota 55439. Copyright © 2024 by Abdo Consulting Group, Inc. International copyrights reserved in all countries. No part of this book may be reproduced in any form without written permission from the publisher. SportsZone™ is a trademark and logo of Abdo Publishing.

Printed in the United States of America, North Mankato, Minnesota.
102023
012024

Cover Photo: Jamison Swift
Interior Photos: Jamison Swift, 4–5, 6, 10, 13, 16, 18–19, 29; Red Line Editorial, 8; Brian Peterson/Minneapolis Star Tribune/ZUMA Press Inc/Alamy, 11, 23, 24–25, 27; Jarod Opperman/The Bulletin/AP Images, 14; Shutterstock Images, 21

Editor: Steph Giedd
Series Designer: Cynthia Della-Rovere

Library of Congress Control Number: 2023939859

Publisher's Cataloging-in-Publication Data

Names: Hewson, Anthony K., author.
Title: Arrowhead 135 / by Anthony K. Hewson
Other title: Arrowhead One Hundred Thirty-five
Description: Minneapolis, Minnesota: Abdo Publishing, 2024 | Series: Extreme sports events | Includes online resources and index.
Identifiers: ISBN 9781098292324 (lib. bdg.) | ISBN 9798384910268 (ebook)
Subjects: LCSH: Extreme sports--Juvenile literature. | Action sports (Extreme sports)--Juvenile literature. | Ultra-marathon running--Juvenile literature. | Running races--Juvenile literature. | All terrain bicycling--Juvenile literature. | Skis and skiing--Juvenile literature. | Winter sports--Juvenile literature.
Classification: DDC 796.046--dc23

TABLE OF CONTENTS

CHAPTER 1
One with Nature 4

CHAPTER 2
Training for the Trail 12

CHAPTER 3
A Winter's Tale 18

CHAPTER 4
The Run to Tower................. 24

Glossary 30
More Information...............31
Online Resources 31
Index..................................32
About the Author 32

CHAPTER 1

ONE WITH NATURE

It was before dawn on a January morning in International Falls, Minnesota, just across the Rainy River from Canada. Athletes shuffled nervously while waiting for the start of one of the world's toughest ultramarathons. Some brave competitors were on bikes, some were on skis, and still others were using their own two feet.

Cyclist Bonnie Moebeck, a 45-year-old originally from Newport Beach, California, was set to compete in the Arrowhead 135 for the first time. The race is a 135-mile (217-km) event held in the frigid northern Minnesota winter. Moebeck was lucky; the temperature for the start of her race was well above zero.

Racers anxiously await the start of the 2022 Arrowhead 135 race.

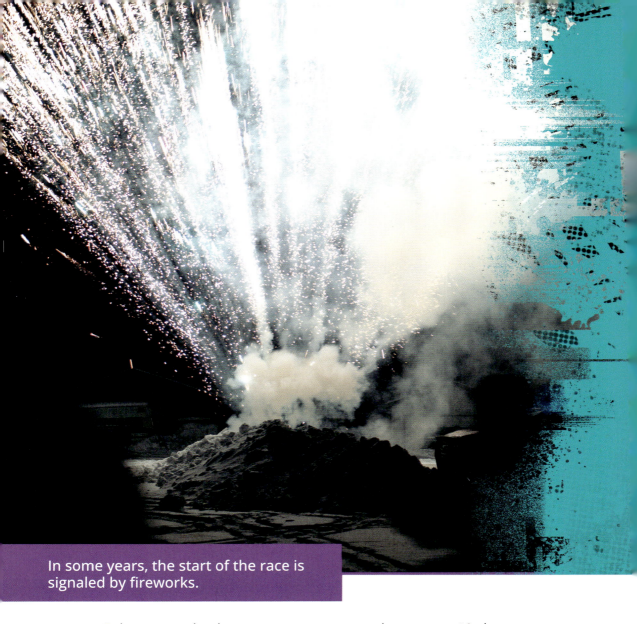

In some years, the start of the race is signaled by fireworks.

Other races had seen temperatures plunge to −40 degrees Fahrenheit (−40°C).

A gunshot into the Minnesota sky signaled the start of the race. Moebeck took off, her bike's wide winter tires pushing the soft snow out of the way. She had just a headlamp and her bike's headlight to guide her. They formed a tunnel of light leading her through the woods.

The field in an Arrowhead race is small, limited to approximately 200 entries. Moebeck soon found herself alone. She had only the sound of the snow under her tires for company. The Arrowhead is a race of solitude, pitting athletes against nature.

The snow continued to fall. And heavy snow made Moebeck's race incredibly difficult. She had to push her bike through wintry conditions for eight hours. Mechanical problems then made it impossible. Moebeck's bike lost all but one of its gears between the first and second checkpoint. She was disappointed to have to drop out due to something beyond her control.

Moebeck was not alone. In a typical year, roughly half of Arrowhead entrants finish. In Moebeck's year, only 36 percent made it to the finish line. That level of difficulty is one reason why the Arrowhead is considered one of the 50 toughest races in the world.

THE RACE TO TOWER

The city of International Falls is known as "the Icebox of the Nation." It regularly features some of the coldest temperatures in the United States throughout the winter. But the coldest temperature ever recorded

ARROWHEAD 135

Rainy Lake

CANADA

International Falls

Namakan Lake

MINNESOTA

1st checkpoint
(Gateway General Store)

Kabetogama Lake

2nd checkpoint
(Melgeorge's Resort)

Pelican Lake

3rd checkpoint

Lake Vermilion

Fortune Bay Casino

Tower

CANADA

MINNESOTA

Lake Superior

WISCONSIN

Racers stop at checkpoints, *blue dots*, to refuel their bodies, make bike repairs, and get out of the cold for a while.

in Minnesota history happened in the city of Tower, where the Arrowhead finish line sits. The area is an incredibly challenging environment in which to hold an ultramarathon.

The first Arrowhead race was held in 2005. Only 10 people signed up for the challenge. Today, the entries are limited to ensure the course does not become too crowded. The race takes place along the Arrowhead Trail.

When the trail is not being used as a racecourse, people enjoy hiking, biking, skiing, snowmobiling, and even horseback riding along its 135 miles. The trail is especially rugged in winter and can become packed with deep snow, which makes it very difficult to navigate.

In some ultramarathons, racers can have pacing runners or support crews giving them supplies. But no outside help is allowed during the Arrowhead 135. Racers must carry their supplies or drag them behind on a sled.

The list of needed supplies is long. Among the items the race recommends is a whistle, to be worn around the neck in case athletes need to call for help. The official race guidelines remind athletes that their mouth may become "too numb to yell" for help in the cold.

THE TOUGHEST YEAR

The 2014 race was a particularly cold year at the Arrowhead, and that showed up in the statistics. An all-time low 33 percent of racers finished. The fastest time was men's bike champion Jay Petervary at a little over 20 hours. His finish was just the fourth time the winner finished in 20 or more hours in race history. On average, most men's bike champions finish in just over 17 hours.

There are only a few places for racers to receive more supplies or help. All racers must stop at three checkpoints. The first is Gateway, a small convenience store 35 miles

Racers must carry their supplies with them, but they can pick up more at the three checkpoints if needed.

(56 km) from the start. Racers can rest, purchase supplies, or make repairs to their equipment. The next stop is another 35 miles down the trail at Melgeorge's Resort.

Racers do whatever they can to keep warm in the frigid northern Minnesota winter.

There, race organizers provide food and water. Racers can even stop to sleep if they want.

The final checkpoint is at the 110-mile (177-km) mark, a small campsite for a quick stop. From there, racers push on to the finish at the Fortune Bay Casino in Tower. If competitors have not reached each checkpoint by a certain time, they will be disqualified. And they have a 60-hour limit to finish the entire race.

Those who finish find themselves in an exclusive club. As of the 2023 edition, there had been just 1,159 finishers in total. And the number of unique finishers is even lower. Many finishers are repeat competitors who can't get enough of one of the world's toughest races.

CHAPTER 2

TRAINING FOR THE TRAIL

The Arrowhead 135 is only for elite athletes. Anyone wanting to enter must fill out an application. Athletes who have entered the race before are given priority, as they have already met the race's high standards for qualification.

Cyclists must have completed either a 200-mile (320-km) road race or a 100-mile (160-km) off-road race. Runners and skiers must have completed a 100-mile race. Winter races carry more value in the application process. Applicants who don't meet these requirements must demonstrate some other experience showing they can safely complete the race. These requirements ensure that athletes have the physical capabilities needed to complete a race with Arrowhead 135's frigid weather conditions.

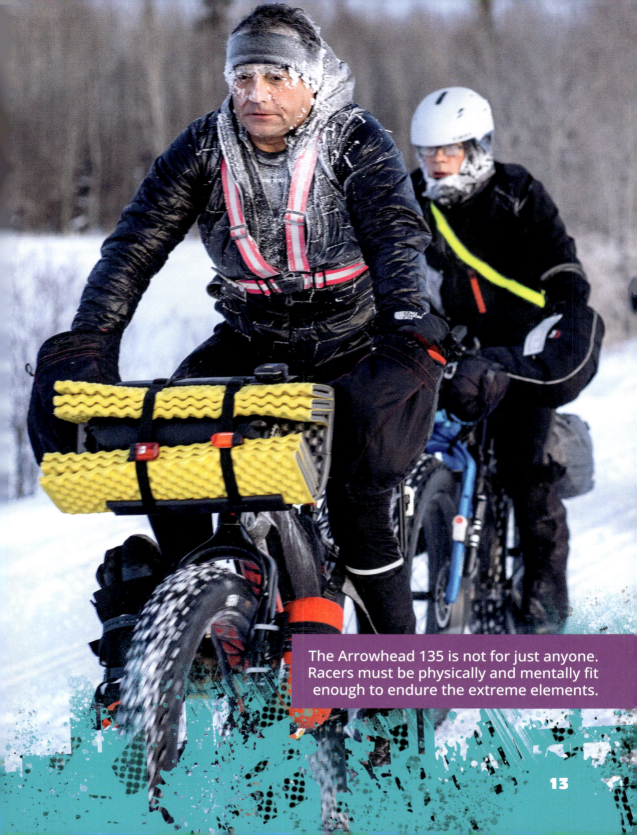

The Arrowhead 135 is not for just anyone. Racers must be physically and mentally fit enough to endure the extreme elements.

13

Chris and Helen Scotch prepare for the Arrowhead 135 by trekking with their gear through Wanoga Snow Park near Bend, Oregon.

Those who compete in the race must also pay an entry fee. Entry for the 2023 race cost $200.

It is difficult to replicate the conditions of the race in training. Bill Bradley, who attempted his 11th Arrowhead in 2023, is from California. His runs along the Pacific coast are nothing like what he sees in Minnesota. But by ramping up to 18-mile (29-km) training runs just weeks before the race, he builds confidence that he has the physical capabilities to run the Arrowhead.

Other athletes have found more extreme preparation methods. Cyclist Sveta Vold was the women's champion in the bike category in 2018. The Minnesota resident takes a plunge into a frozen lake each winter, which she believes helps build endurance and acclimates her to the cold for the race.

PACKING LIST

A major part of preparing for the Arrowhead is having all the necessary gear. Since racers don't have a support crew, they must bring everything they need along with them. And it's a lot of gear.

The race requires certain items. Even with the most experienced ultramarathoners on Earth, race organizers take no chances on safety. Every athlete must have a satellite tracking device since they spend much of their time out on the course alone.

There are plenty of other safety items. Racers need to have a sleeping bag that can handle temperatures of −20 degrees Fahrenheit (−29°C) or colder. They must carry some kind of tent in order to properly camp if needed. And they must carry a stove, food, and water.

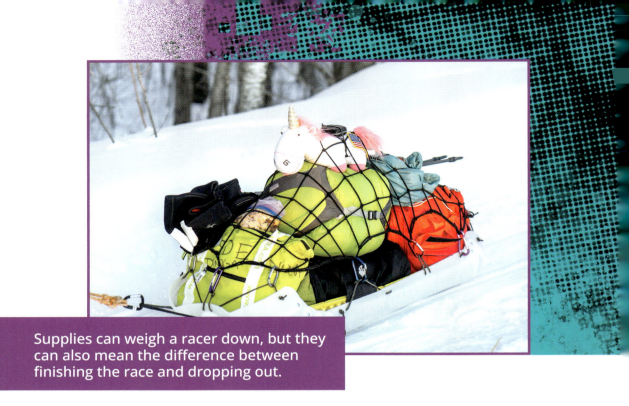

Supplies can weigh a racer down, but they can also mean the difference between finishing the race and dropping out.

The Arrowhead is an endurance race, but it's also a test of winter survival skills. Veteran Arrowhead racer John Storkamp believes that a great camper is likely to have more success in the race than an elite marathoner. Before one of his Arrowhead attempts, Bradley arrived early in International Falls to practice setting up his camp. He didn't want his first time setting up the equipment under the harsh winter conditions to be while the race was underway, when he would be extremely tired.

Other required items include front and rear lights, an insulated sleeping pad, a fire starter, and more. And then there are plenty of other items some racers may choose to bring, such as extra layers of clothes or extra equipment.

Skiers may bring an extra set of skis, and runners may bring snowshoes. But any gear or clothing a racer starts with must still be with them when they cross the finish line.

How racers carry their gear is up to them. The gear can weigh 25 pounds (11.3 kg) or more, so a backpack can weigh a racer down. Cyclists can strap their gear to racks on their bikes. Many runners and skiers opt to tow their gear behind them on a sled.

There are also race officials checking to make sure racers have all the required gear. And they check again at the finish line to ensure that racers still have the required supplies. For example, racers must carry a one-day supply of food at all times, including when they cross the finish line. If they don't have the required supplies, racers can be disqualified. Only those who come prepared will be able to finish.

CHAPTER 3

A WINTER'S TALE

Competitors say that no two Arrowheads are alike. The course is the same, but the conditions vary wildly each year. And there is no accounting for when a mechanical or equipment problem can crop up.

Runner John Storkamp's experiences serve as an example of the volatility of the race. He won the entire footrace in 2006, 2008, 2011, and 2018. But he failed to finish in 2009 and 2012. The race tests even its most successful entrants.

Athletes need to know the effect of snow and cold on their performance. This makes previous winter ultramarathon experience incredibly valuable. No matter how good some athletes are, they won't be able to keep up their

Racers can complete the race on a bike, on skis, or on foot. The weather can bring challenges to racers no matter their chosen mode of transportation.

A TOUGH WAY TO GO

Skiing the Arrowhead is especially difficult. Trail conditions can deteriorate rapidly and are rarely ideal for skiing. As of the 2023 race, just 44 of the 1,159 all-time Arrowhead finishers were skiers. Only four skiers attempted it in 2023, and none of them finished.

usual pace in Arrowhead conditions. If they try, they'll only overwork themselves, and that can be dangerous. The more athletes work, the more they sweat. And moisture in frigid conditions can cool the body rapidly. A condition called hypothermia occurs when the body temperature gets too low, and it's a real threat during the Arrowhead. It can lead to death if a person doesn't get warm soon enough.

Too much moisture can cause other problems as well, such as blisters. Additionally, frostbite is a common and serious problem during this race. Frostbite occurs when a person's skin is exposed to freezing temperatures for too long. The skin and tissue just below the skin freeze, which can cause long-term damage. Signs of frostbite include numbness, swelling, and discolored skin.

FIGHTING THROUGH CHALLENGES

As athletes get tired, they move more slowly. They spend more time out on the course instead of getting to a

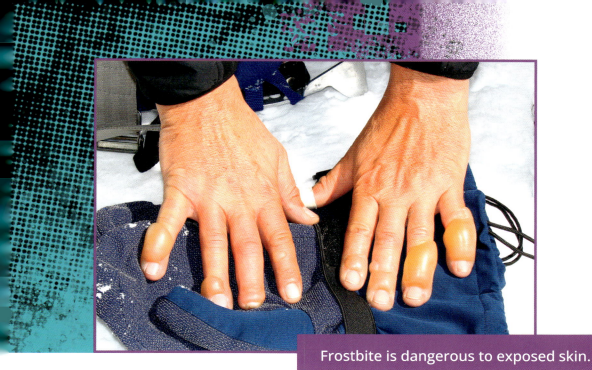

Frostbite is dangerous to exposed skin.

checkpoint. If they get so tired that they need to rest before reaching the next checkpoint, they might have to set up their own camps along the trail. This adds more time to their races. And there are consequences for not making a checkpoint. Once racers arrive at a checkpoint, they can stay as long as they wish. However, all racers must leave each checkpoint by a specific time during the three days of the race. If they haven't, they are out of the race. Anyone who hasn't yet entered a checkpoint by its designated time is also out of the race.

The Arrowhead is mentally draining as well as physically taxing. Many veteran racers say keeping themselves going is one of the hardest parts of the race. And there is no way to train for the mental part of it.

Athletes push their bodies to the limit, and sometimes their bodies push back. Racers often report seeing things that aren't there when they get totally exhausted. Racer Charlie Farrow once said that at about 20 hours into the race, he starts to have visions of trees chasing him like the ones in *The Wizard of Oz*.

Racers often turn to each other for support. Those moving at a similar pace may opt to stay together for conversation. It can help to keep the mental exhaustion at bay.

Athletes are allowed to help each other on the course. They can share supplies but cannot ever be without any of their own required gear. Ultimately, the Arrowhead is a race to be completed solo.

If a mechanical problem arises, there are few ways to overcome it. Even if a cyclist is carrying equipment to fix a problem, the cold can make it nearly impossible to make the repair. Just as for Bonnie Moebeck in 2013, a broken bike often means the end of the race.

Many times, racers find themselves alone on the trail. It takes a lot of focus to keep going.

CHAPTER 4

THE RUN TO TOWER

P art of the mental challenge of the Arrowhead is simply its length. It takes a lot of concentration to stay focused for 135 miles (217 km). By the time racers reach the final checkpoint, only 25 miles (40 km) remain. But many racers have already pushed themselves to the limit by that point. The third and final checkpoint is where they make their final push—or call it quits.

In 2013 Oscar Schefers was exhausted. He waited at the last checkpoint for five hours, hoping maybe he'd see a snowmobile—a race official to pull him off the course once he dropped out. But seeing none, he decided it would be faster to just get back on his bike and finish the race.

Athletes must pack items such as lights, reflectors, and headlamps in order to continue competing at night.

25

The same year, Morgan Porath wasn't able to find the same push to continue. Porath arrived at the checkpoint feeling ill and unable to eat. After resting for a few hours, he ended his race.

The 25-mile stretch to the finish is fairly flat, with one big exception. There is one final hill known as "Wakemup Hill." The elevation change leaves racers exposed to heavy winds as they make one last push. Once they make it to the top, however, they're treated to a scenic view of the forest below, stretching out for miles.

ITS OWN REWARD

After making the final approach to the finish line, exhausted and excited racers may finally relax. There are no gold medals or big cash prizes for finishing. As the Arrowhead 135 website states, the reward is the "satisfaction of finishing one of [the] hardest ultra events in North America/the world."

However, a few awards are given out for notable finishes. Finishing the Arrowhead is hard enough, but athletes also have an option to run the race "unsupported." That means racers receive no help whatsoever—no use of the shelter, food, or water available at checkpoints. The category was first introduced in 2017, and by 2023 only 141 racers had finished unsupported. Those who accomplish this feat receive a special trophy shaped like an arrowhead.

Though the race is challenging, it is full of beautiful winter views.

    There are other awards given for perseverance and for helping other racers on the course. There is also the "Arrowhead à Trois" award for athletes who have finished the race in all three disciplines in their careers. As of 2023, only 22 racers had earned this award.

Finishing the Arrowhead is difficult, but biking is statistically the easiest way to do it. More bikers finish the race than any other group—70 percent. It's also the fastest way down the trail. Jordan Wakeley set the race record in 2019, finishing in a time of 11 hours, 43 minutes.

However the race is run, it's a memorable experience. Even those who do not finish have a desire to return and try again another year. The challenge of the race is what keeps everyone coming back.

JUST A NUMBER

Racers who attempt the Arrowhead tend to be older, more experienced athletes. Erv Berglund ran the Arrowhead for the first time at age 69 in 2012. He became the oldest person to finish the race in 2014. He then beat his own record by finishing the 2018 race at the age of 75.

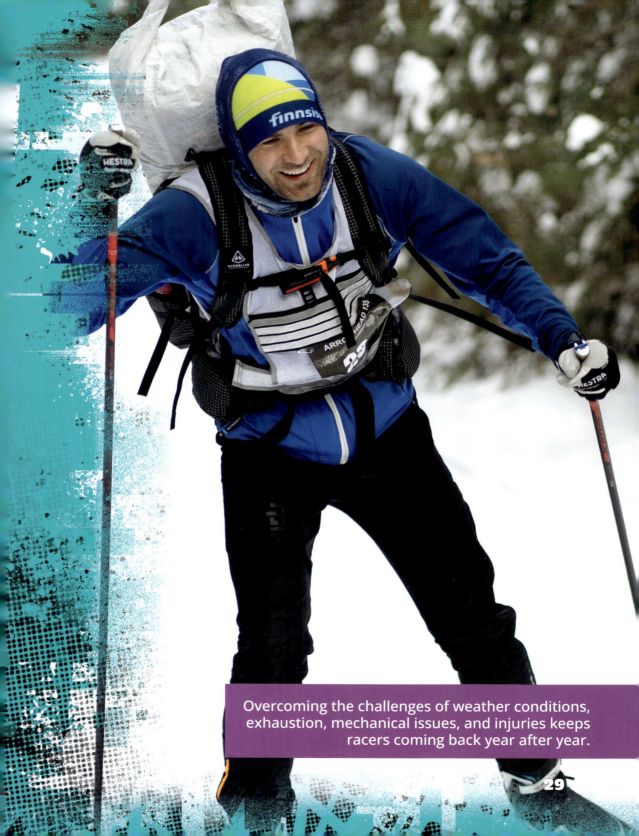

Overcoming the challenges of weather conditions, exhaustion, mechanical issues, and injuries keeps racers coming back year after year.

GLOSSARY

checkpoint
A stop along the way within a larger course.

disciplines
Different areas of study or expertise.

elevation
The distance above sea level.

elite
Among the best at something.

endurance
The quality of being able to do something for a long time.

entrants
People who have entered into a competition.

frigid
Extremely cold.

pace
The speed at which an athlete progresses through a race.

rugged
Rough or unrefined.

solitude
The state of being alone.

ultramarathon
A race lasting longer than the standard marathon distance of 26.2 miles.

volatility
The tendency to be unpredictable.

MORE INFORMATION

BOOKS

Hanlon, Luke. *Iditarod Trail Invitational*. Minneapolis, MN: Abdo Publishing, 2024.

Hogan, Christa C. *Mountain Biking*. Minneapolis, MN: Abdo Publishing, 2020.

Vernon, Jane. *Minnesota*. Minneapolis, MN: Abdo Publishing, 2023.

ONLINE RESOURCES

To learn more about the Arrowhead 135, please visit **abdobooklinks.com** or scan this QR code. These links are routinely monitored and updated to provide the most current information available.

31

INDEX

Arrowhead à Trois award, 27
Arrowhead Trail, 8–9

Berglund, Erv, 28
Bradley, Bill, 14, 16

Farrow, Charlie, 22
Fortune Bay Casino, 11
frostbite, 20

Gateway, 9–10

hypothermia, 20

International Falls, Minnesota, 4, 7, 16

Melgeorge's Resort, 10–11
Moebeck, Bonnie, 4–7, 22

Petervary, Jay, 9
Porath, Morgan, 26

Schefers, Oscar, 24
Storkamp, John, 16, 18

Tower, Minnesota, 8, 11

Vold, Sveta, 15

Wakeley, Jordan, 28
Wakemup Hill, 26

ABOUT THE AUTHOR

Anthony K. Hewson is a freelance writer originally from San Diego. He and his wife now live in the San Francisco Bay Area with their two dogs.